IT'S A *Walking* TESTIMONY

Sharon Outland

WESTBOW®
PRESS
A DIVISION OF THOMAS NELSON
& ZONDERVAN

WestBow Press books may be ordered through booksellers or by contacting:

WestBow Press
A Division of Thomas Nelson & Zondervan
1663 Liberty Drive
Bloomington, IN 47403
www.westbowpress.com
1 (866) 928-1240

ISBN: 978-1-4908-6431-0 (sc)

Library of Congress Control Number: 2014922622

Printed in the United States of America.

WestBow Press rev. date: 01/23/2015

Contents

The Reason

The Elevation

Acknowledgements

IT'S
A WALKING
TESTIMONY

BY

SHARON OUTLAND

Thy word is a lamp unto my feet, and a
light unto my path. Psalms 119:105

Thanks to all family and friends for the love and show
of support during our trying times, A Special Thanks to
Patrice having you there made a world of difference!

Expectation

Overcoming the Obstacles
Patience of the Missionary
A mind in Jesus
Jubilee Season

1

"Overcome the Obstacles"

It was March 15th 1998; all was well on a routine Sunday. Our family were doing fine, the children were ok, a loving husband great father and provider; all seemed well in our home everything was at its best. On that day our lives changed forever. All eyes were on me! How can I handle the pain and the loss? In a moment of a twinkling of an eye sadness surrounded our household. I can remember reading an article some time ago which talked about the darkest hour was just before the dawn, but for me and my children that dark hour came at 4:30pm in the afternoon on a bright and lovely sunny day. The Lord called Martinez home; that was the day in our life. Could we survive? Could we be strong?

Martinez was out putting gas in the cars and making sure finances were in order for that week, when he returned home, he was complaining of chest pains and wanted to lay down. Instead he was taken to the hospital. On his arrival, he stated that he could not make it any further. The medical staff ran to him and took over. While I was waiting I began Praying to the Lord about my husband. I just wanted him to get better and come home, but the Lord decided.

Oh! Oh! Oh! What a day, what a time in our life. In the still of the night; I was awaken by the tears and whispers of cries and Love for a daddy who had to say good-bye to those who loved him so very much.

The sounds of our children Sharonica, Octavia, and Adrian echoes added through the night, much to my sorrow and pain. We lay in bed together children are all around, Sharonica was crying, Adrian wrap around my waist and Octavia at the foot of the bed holding on to my ankle. As I held On to my Faith in God, for the battle was not mine it's the Lords.

Thinking about the word of God, I'm reminded of the disciples in the fourth chapter of Mark, when they was crossing over to the other side and a great windstorm came and Jesus was there on board with them and calmed the sea. Just as the storms rages in our lives, Know that Jesus cares for all of us.

We are Gods children. I invited Jesus in that night, I sat up in bed stretched out my hands and said these words. "In the mighty name of Jesus, Peace be still." The Lord met me right where I was a weeping Widow, he brought a peace only God could bring a quietness that calmed the house; until a faucet five feet away dripped and I heard it. Talk about calming a raging sea, he will walk, talk, comfort, protect and keep you. Never leaving you alone, he will always be there.

I wanted to make it, I wanted to survive, I wanted to pull through and with the help of the Lord I will. I remember being at the hospital, I just wanted to hide myself'; I didn't want anyone to notice me and see the shape I was in. I walked out of the glass exit door and stood behind it. I watched the Doctors and Nurses look for me, but they couldn't see me. They were right there and I wasn't found. In Psalms 27:5 Gods words states "He shall hide me in his secret place". I walked through the glass doors and was seen.

God carried me, I had to have the strength only God could give and the faith the size of a mustard seed' because this was my mountain in my life. I had to face it. His love was what I needed his comfort it was to protect and keep me step by step all the way he carried me through.

I had to raise a son without a father, but God said he'll be a father to the fatherless. I thank god for his Mercy and Grace toward me, having two daughters well I know his Grace is sufficient "Hallelujah". Starting a new life ahead wasn't easy; I was angry and bitter because it all happened to me. I didn't want this position, but I had no choice; I was here. The shoe's I was wearing was much too large, but the comfort of God allows me to walk with the promise that he will never leave me nor forsakes me. He will be there till the end. Revelations 21:7 "He who over comes shall inherit all things I have a brand new walk with God", my conversation is different; I want the words of my mouth to expectable in thy sight. God has changed my life, I'm not bitter anymore; just better at serving God. Because of what he has done, I choose to worship him.

I realize his goodness; I thank him for his greatness and the magnitude of his love. I continue to walk this path called life, remembering what brought me here and who kept us all. I am more than a conqueror through Jesus Christ, sharing the love of God.

Walking in Faith as God is our tomorrow.

"Patience of the Missionary"

When I was a young girl, I was always told that we are to see Jesus in everything. This is my testimony....

My experience at a Nail Boutique led me to this passage of scripture; James 1:4 which reads, "But let patience have its perfect work that you may be perfect and complete, lacking nothing, walk in faith if you will. Entering into the Nail Boutique, finding all stations busy, all I wanted was my Nails to be filled.

"How long is the wait?" I thought.

"Will it be in a moment, or in the twinkling of an eye? I'm in a hurry and time is winding up? Who am I waiting on?"

I am waiting on the Lord and as I sit waiting the world does not stop turning. The happenings continue on in God's perfect plan. I'd received a certificate from the Nail Boutique for my Birthday, and I had no idea that it was about to expire. So after I got off work, I went straight there. When I arrived, there were only four stations I signed in and asked, how long will it take? The nail tech replies, "Have a seat please, it won't be long." As I sat looking around, I heard the many different conversations; sick children, the news, getting married and promises being made.

Finally, it was my turn. I sat down at the first station and the tech began to work on my nails. I noticed everyone was leaving out at the same time. I was the only one left, and I wanted to go too. Matthew 19:30 encourages us stating,"... many that are first shall be last; and the last shall be first." The tech that started out working with me had done all she was going to do. Then the head tech of the nail shop came over to do the rest. As I was looking around, I saw everyone cleaning their station.

I got a little anxious because I was the last one, and it was getting late. Now ready to leave, the tech that started out working on me came and sat by my side. She reassured me that everything would be all right, and it won't be much longer. It reminded me of the Holy Spirit letting us know that no matter what we feel or go through he will always be there to comfort us.

The work was complete, and the tech walked around and stood behind me. When I got up, I bumped the table and messed up a nail. He walked over to see the damage and came back with his repair tools. I said, "It's ok! I know you do good work it won't be a reflection on your shop!" He responds, "Stay! I want to fix it up for you."

I thought it was on one hand, and it was both. Thinking about the word of God, when we get in a hurry it says that "the race is not to the swift, nor the battle to the strong, neither yet bread to the wise, nor yet riches to men of understanding, nor yet favor to men of skill, but time and chance happen to them all." The Spirit of the Lord will lead and guide us, even if we think we're ready, his word says, Humble yourselves, therefore, under the mighty hand of God that he may exalt you in due time. Being a vessel that God can use requires a change and from that moment on, I walked out in the newness.

As I'm thinking about my experience I had at the Nail Boutique, the scripture James 1:4 came in my spirit and for me it was the makings of the missionary. We go through storms in life, and don't understand, but recognize that God has a purpose. When we come in contact with the master, we're no longer the same. We're changed individuals, and now Gods plan can work in our lives like never before. His timing is always perfect and right. There is no secret to what God can do. What he has done for many others he will do for you. Some have walked away too soon from an opportunity to be blessed by God because they didn't wait.

Isaiah 40:31 "But those that wait on the Lord, Shall renew their strength; they shall mount up with wings like eagles; they shall run and not be weary; they shall walk and not faint." Wait on the Lord be of good cheer, and he will strengthen your heart!" When God puts the finishing touches and enlightens our lives, we will shine as bright as a morning star.

We will walk by faith and not by sight, leaning and trusting in Gods holy word.

You can say to those who saw and knew you in times of trouble that you made it through another's day's journey. It was God that kept you. We all have experienced our share of heartaches trials and disappointments. We're here because God has allowed us to be.

When God brings you through trials, share and help someone else to make it out. Tell them even though broken-hearted God can repair it. Share your testimony and let them know. Out of everything we must go through God still loves us, and we need to understand that he really cares. After writing the patients of the missionary, I sat up in bed and gasp, "Oh Lord am I the missionary?" Yes, I am.

"A Mind in Jesus"

The Lord is the ultimate source of; strength and power, mind body and soul. Devastating moments or events can impact your life permanently. When you lose a loved one, a job, or even friendships, you may feel as though you have lost everything. Dwelling on the past can cloud your judgment. We panic, fall apart, get lost in confusion, and are consumed. However, the way out is through Jesus Christ, he'll never leave you.

When disturbing news comes it's like a ton of brick thrown through a glass window, it can shatter the mind! You can't eat, sleep, or think! Sometimes you can't tell whether you're going or coming. Imagine you just lost a house, possessions, or close relationship. Things can get to be so strong it will make us feel as though we're losing our mind.

I remember standing at the door from six o'clock until eight o'clock every evening. Waiting for my husband, but after a while I knew he wasn't coming back. My sister would come to the door and ask what's out there or what was I looking to see. I shifted my shoulders shaking my head and walked away with a smile deep within, thinking if she knew. The mind can play terrible tricks on you. It's so easy to assume one thing, so you won't have to deal with the truth. Telling yourself he's on assignment and temporary duty that's why he hasn't made it home.

It doesn't matter who you are or how strong minded you may be it can happen to you. God has the power to strengthen the mind and care for a broken spirit; he says "He's a present help in the time of trouble".

Lord I need you! There are moments in my life right now that I can't seem to face, but I don't want to give up. You see I watch my husband take his last breath, it was a hurting experience. I reasoned that I could make it, but only if God be there with me. Others might say that; my mind got lost. Still, it takes knowing God for yourself and understanding if God is for you he's more than the world against you. All is well in our loving Father's hands. You don't lose the mind you make changes to accommodate your situation. Philippians 2:5 tell us to "Let this mind be in you which was also in Christ Jesus!" People's opinions are just what they are, opinions! They don't mean anything; they don't know your story.

One afternoon I decided to go to the grocery store. When I made it on the inside, I was stopped by a fellow patron. Someone asked if I got my mind back after losing my husband. Do you know he's a way maker? Be encouraged! The God I serve kept my mind one hundred percent! Isaiah twenty-six and three affirms that, "thou with keep him in perfect peace whose mind is stayed on thee because he trust in thee." Just because you have difficult moments in your life or experience a change that bring you down during trying times; this doesn't mean that you get out of control and get disconnected from God and his word. I'm a witness we all have a breaking point. Nevertheless, God is our refuge and strength, he hears and answers prayer. I can't thank God enough for directing the road I was on. He sustained me; the Lord made the difference, hallelujah!

I wasn't on medication, hospitalized, institutionalized, or incarcerated. It was Gods wondrous working power of the Holy Spirit that took control. He protected me and kept me safe from all harm, and kept me clothed in my right mind.

God specializes in those things that are rough and rocky; that makes life seem so unbearable. He has the power! I know! He has done what no man or other power could do and transitioned me to the next level. Take the steps to walk in his word and make him your own. Trust him, keep the faith, and stay strong. Let his word abide in you and you in him, and whatever desire you may have, he will give to you. Whatever it is, give it to Jesus, the mind, body, and soul ask for help, he'll be there. Ephesians 3:20 Now unto him that is able to do exceeding abundantly, above all that we ask or think, according to the power that worketh in us.

"The Jubilee Season"

One day while visiting my mother I fell asleep on her couch. Just before I opened my eyes to wake, I heard this scripture "Psalm133." I woke up, hopped off the couch, and got all my things together to go home. When I arrived there, I grabbed my bible, eager to read and interpret this scripture's meaning. It read, "Behold how good and how pleasant it is for brethren to dwell together in unity." That alone spoke to me! I had separated myself from my family and friends, and it took God's word to help me. As I finished reading this scripture, I referred to some back up scriptures to support this found in Deuteronomy chapter four. The basis of discussion plainly and clearly focused on the children of Israel and their deliverance from captivity.

I said to myself, "Oh Lord! After all this time, you're bringing me out? It's seven long years." Leviticus 25:21, also one of my back up scriptures, supported this by declaring, "I will command my blessings on you." The Jubilee year is a time for celebration. In my youth, I heard about the seven years limit on debts that they were cleared, but never had I heard of a Jubilee!

I began to think about the things that were missing in my life. I told my children to get ready for a Jubilee season because we were about to experience a change! We were all excited. My family asked who's included. I said those that stayed with me during the time of my storm. In the excitement, I called and shared the vision with many others. I exclaimed it could be materialistic, health and wealth! Don't lose sight of where you came from! Stay in Gods will and line up in the word.

I was home relaxing one evening, and the phone rang. It was my mother on the other end saying come quickly! I asked, "What going on?", as I hurried over. Everyone was rejoicing over a financial blessing and thanking God. I asked the question "Is anyone believing?" They all shouted "Yes!" I always heard that seeing is believing. I now know in order to receive, you must believe. My sister walks in one day and says come see my new car! We all rejoiced with her. Later that evening I sat down on the couch and started to wonder about my blessings. Where are they? Wasn't I the one who had the vision?"

As time went by I thought less and less about the Jubilee year, but God has a way of reminding us of his promises. I sent my daughter to the store for decorations for the bathroom and she came back with Jubilee Cherubs! I thought as I laughed, "Ha Ha Ha," thinking how awesome is my God. I made sure that nothing stood in the way to keep me from receiving my blessings.

Anything in my life that wasn't of God I left it alone. I trusted God to do just what he said he would, and he brought me out of my wilderness.

I started walking in the light of his word, putting my faith and trust in him, and expecting my blessings. That's when he restored my joy. I'm so happy that God favored me. I praise him because I know him; no rock needs to cry out for me. After all these tears I've shed, my hands are waving in the air. I'm jumping for joy. I'm shouting and doing my dance, Hallelujah! I'm restored, and I'm getting my praise on. When my husband departed this life, I lost my security. There was no one to look to. No one could measure up. I was searching high and low and couldn't find anyone. I found the love of our Lord and savior Jesus Christ. His word covered me and held me close. God has been my protector. Make no mistake about it; he is my blessing and the only one that can sooth my soul.

Physical strength was lost and I was weak. I didn't feel like driving, cooking, or getting dressed.

In all you can stand. In God, old things are passed away and behold all things are made new. You are restored! You will be put back together again! I had a family who stood by me through the thick and the thin. They showed their love and support and helped me pull through! I didn't give up. There is freedom in the word of God! Will he make away? "YES he will!" Did he do it for me? "Yes he did!" When you're down and out, struggling to get through and can't find your way. Just trust God to send his word, stand on it, and you'll have all you need, be blessed.

Confident

The Graciousness of God
God's Grace is Sufficient
Peace Be Still
Walk into Your Season

"The Graciousness of God"

It was early one Sunday morning, as I lay in bed half asleep, I drifted off and heard "the graciousness of God!" I hopped up, stumbling to find my notebook and pen to write this down just in case I couldn't remember when I got back up. When thinking about these moments, the memories flood my mind. I reflected on how powerful God is, and merciful, in sustaining my family and myself as we underwent the events of that dreadful day.

Withholding nothing, he shows his love and kindness toward us all. God strengthen me that I might see and know for myself how it all happened and what took place. God covered us and kept us from a place of wondering to give peace in the midst of the storm. I was shocked and devastated, thinking if it had not been for the Lord on my side I would wonder about that today. Martinez and I were together when it happened, and that was truly a blessing from God. We were seeing one another not knowing or thinking it may be the last time. I recall the comforts that no one had to call or knock on our door. As we were talking my husband said to me, "Don't worry everything will be alright." At these words, we held hands as usual; just as we had any other time when we would face changes in life.

We'd faced many adverse situations as husband and wife and even in tragedy God show his love regardless of what's taking place. As we waited an outpouring of God's love for a family that needed him, the most was right there. He kept us all strong in a mighty way. Philippians 4:7 informs us that "The peace of God, which passes all understanding, shall keep your hearts and minds through Christ Jesus."

As we traveled home from vacation, his graciousness was no accidental occurrence on the road. God just didn't see fit to let it be. Martinez had taken ill the next day. I'm encouraged by God's graciousness and the peaceful mind he has given to me. The Lord never leaves us to wonder about his graciousness, but lets us know he is gracious.

"My Grace is Sufficient"

One summer evening I was sitting in the recliner watching television, and I decided to work on the computer. In comes my niece. She sits down in a chair beside me, and she coughs. I looked over at her to kid around and play and as I was playing the cough started to worsen. Concerned, I said stop coughing like that your coughing too hard, and I don't want you to cough up anything. Well, in came the sad face, so I picked her up, plus I knew she wasn't feeling well. I put her on my shoulder to pat her almost instantly the cough stopped, and that's when I heard my grace is sufficient. I began to think about what happened. We all act like children at times, uncomfortable with our conditions and surroundings. As a result, we get sick, stressed, and depressed needlessly to say. The love of God quickens our spirit and helps to calm us down when things go wrong. Embrace every moment of God's love and hold him tight. God doesn't want us to do anything that will inflict harm upon us. I remember when I would lay in bed and sleep all day with no desire to eat. Most times I would eat a bite here and there, and although my family was there with me, I was still very weak. I had to have a strong touch from God. I was carrying things that weighed heavy and strong on my mind. In my life I needed God's help, he revealed himself in Matthew 11:28-29 saying, "Come unto to me, all ye that labor and are heavy laden, and I will give you rest.

19

Take my yoke upon you, and learn of me; for I am meek and lowly in heart: and ye shall find rest unto your souls. My yoke is easy, and my burden is light."

God's grace is sufficient it is enough, and it's all you'll ever need. God moved in my life and made the load a lot lighter. He placed people in the lives of my children to encourage them. When I couldn't see the need my sisters would do things from time to time to help me out by making sure my children were cared for. I can't imagine what my life would have been like without the love of the Lord Jesus on my side working through others just for me. When I think about God and how he saved my life, I'm considering how tall he stands over me saying; run on my daughter I'm running with you every step of the way.

"Peace Be Still"

While getting ready for church, the Sunday school teacher began talking; asking questions and listening. I'm combing my hair; the radio and television are on. I looked at the mirror and turned to the door and heard this whispered, "Peace be still." There are occasions when we get caught up in the middle of the affairs of life, and it makes it difficult to handle at one time. God can't tell us what he wants us to know because were too busy with extra things on our mind. One day when talking with a friend we began discussing how hectic things can get to be in life. I shared what I'd discovered, if you want peace one should make up in his or her mind to go find peace. Remembering the first night that I had become a widow, it was so much happening and too much to handle at that point in my life. We all were crying the kids were saying I want daddy we have no more daddy mama, I can't believe he's really not here anymore, and why did he have to go away? A mother was holding and rocking her children because she knew their hurt. Trying to help them became almost impossible when there was no help for her.

Calling on the peace of God in prayer, he made a swift move and brought about the peace we needed to calm us down when our emotions were running high. When you pray for peace he demonstrates it through the power of his holy spirit. My children were listening and they heard the prayer too and they begin to calm down. I knew if I could pray to Jesus, doors of peace would open up in my household. Living in a world that's changing before your eyes can get pretty stressful. While attempting to maintain peace without God, we may leave our jobs, taking issues into our home, contaminating our families and the life God has given to us. Our marriages suffer and so does our walk with the Lord. We're in violation of the peace from God, John 14:27 assures us that, "Peace I leave with you, my peace I give unto you: not as the world giveth, give I unto you." Speak life in your present condition. Proclaim, "I will have peace on my job, in my home and where ever I may go!" Surround yourself with the peace of God and walk in the authority of his word and maintain serenity. John 15:7 states, "If ye abide in me, and my words abide in you, ye shall ask what ye will, and it shall be done unto you."

"Walk Into Your Season"

I'm walking in the season of promise, stepping out on faith with my steps ordered by the Lord. With every step that I take I realize its Jesus, I understand who I am and to whom I belong. Early morning rising I opened the door to step outside and heard these words, walk into your blessings. I looked out ahead and thought it's my time to experience the blessings of the Lord. Later on in this day I was driving my car, I made a stop at the stop sign, looking both ways and then straight ahead. I thought if God would have drawn himself from me where could I have gone? It amazes me how God orders your steps. The Lord guided me in my sorrow, and he is with me in this tomorrow. He has been my friend, the bright and morning star.

The Almighty was there for me; he is the way, the truth, and the life. Trusting in the Lord has made me glad. I came out of my season of pain with a renewed mind in him as my life long healer. He has kept me! Jehovah has been my protector, provider, and he is my God. He was the only one that was able to keep me from falling. The Lord God showed compassion during this trial of mine. I trusted him, and now he has blessed me beyond measure.

I can speak a word with the authority of God. The potter has made and molded my life. Where I was weak, Our Father has strengthened me and now through him I've been made strong. While he was testing me, he was blessing me and building up my faith and trust in him.

I found out that God could trust me in what I was going through while I had to trust him to get through. God would never put more on me than I could bear. I counted his word to be all he said it would be. The Shepherd of my life and the God of all times. He is the evidence that proves to me that he is my wheel in the middle of a wheel. When I was motionless he kept me moving in the right way, he brought me through, the faithful God I know and serve.

I can be strong now and persevere. I'm on a new level praising his name, for he has chosen me to be a vessel to serve and honor him. An Omnipotent God that showers me with his words of promise. Has given me the opportunity of a lifetime to bless his name, and I thank him. God allows me to glorify him through the Holy Spirit. Matthew 5:16 says "let your light so shine before men, that they may see your good works, and glorify your Father that is in heaven." God has richly blessed me with the knowledge of his word and truth, now I can go to others and talk about the goodness of God.

I can share with so many and identify with those that are having difficulties in dealing with some of the same issues I experienced; especially when it comes to what I have undergone. It saddens my heart when I see others and reminds me where I was and what it was like to feel anxiety and panic attacks. It's like seeing one's self in another's state and being aware of where I used to be. Now, I can encourage others to stand strong in the Lord. Luke 22:32 urges us," But I had prayed for thee, that thy faith fail not: and when thou art converted, strengthen thy brethren." Just knowing the same God that carried me is that same God that will be there for others too. Walk with the assurance of God's word, trust, and believe in him when your back is against the wall. He has saved and wonderfully made me. The Lord has done marvelous works, of his goodness I can testify. I'm thankful and grateful! As I walk, I'm glorifying God daily with the abilities that he has given me.

I'm living a blessed life walking in the blessings and favor of God. He has brought me out in his way and his time. Although he could have chosen to do things differently, instead he chooses to deliver me. Psalms 30:5 reassures believers that, "Weeping may endure for a night, but joy come in the morning. He didn't say how long this night would be; his promise for me was that the joy would come in this morning. In this season, I'm remembering God and with every waking moment and time. I'm enjoying my life once again new thoughts, new dreams, and new attitudes.

"A season of promise is a new beginning in life letting go and grabbing hold to the promise of God that awaits those after the rain."

Strength

It's not Over
I Thirst
In Times Like These
Pull Together
You Got the Victory

"It's Not Over"

It was one afternoon, while standing in a room; I turned and heard these words, "It's not over." I spoke out loud saying "I know it's not over!" I began to think; I have my family, my life, health, strength. I have no doubt that it's not over! After all I'd gone through with Jesus, the rock of ages the foundation of this world, I knew he didn't bring me this far to leave me.

There have been times on this road that it got a little rocky I wasn't sure if I wanted to stay or quit, yet even still I had to stay the course and examine myself. There was no room to quit! I had to make a decision and not give up and throw in the towel! In all of this, I thank God I had family that needed me to be strong. I was devastated, shocked, and hurt; nevertheless as Jesus is Lord he will surely keep me. I have my moments, and I'm finding them to be less and less each day. As I retain those memories of the past, I can be happy and smile about them in this day.

There have been many hills and mountains to climb. Trying to do your best wasn't always easy sometimes it got hard, but I learned to stand in difficult times and conditions. I have to move on now. I can't stay here in sadness any longer the storm that brought me is over! In closing my eyes, I think about the old times, and how much they meant. I have matured, now I can face tomorrow. So much has become spiritual in my life and now I can see the blessings of God.

My children are fully grown now, living their lives and making the best of it. I will always pray to God when I find myself struggling to make it. Even when things happen the way they happen, you discover what you've gone through seems so small when you come out. As I reach beyond the break, I'm holding fast to God's word. In trials and tribulations you can survive, and God is glorified. Matthew 6:34 encourages us to, "Take, therefore, no thought for the morrow: for the morrow shall take thought for the things of itself." I won't worry about the future, I'll just hold on to God's unchanging hand. In the refreshing moments of life, God is our resource.

It makes no difference who you are you can count on the Lord; he is no respect of persons. It's only over if God says it over! In reaping the harvest of a brand new day, open your eyes and receive what's for you. If I can wave my hands and lift my voice, then I can say thank you Jesus. When each storm is over, I welcome the joy it brings. Now, I look in the mirror and see that God has made a change in me. In transforming my life God's given new directions on how to apply his word in trying times. I think about the many years of loss, and how good God has been. Psalms 126:5 tells us, "They that sow in tears shall reap in joy." 1st Corinthians 2:9 asserts, "But it's written, eye hath not seen, nor ear heard, neither have entered into the heart of man, the things that God has prepared for them that love him."

Standing on the word of God, I can expect to receive his blessings. In spite of everything, we go through the spirit of life still dwells. When things happen that we don't understand, we feel like giving up and assume it's over. In spite of difficulty, keep the faith, hold on, and never let go. Don't be quick to draw conclusions to any matter when God is on your side! He will come and confirm to us in many ways that it is not over. Rejoice because God's been good, understand, in all thy ways acknowledge him, and he shall direct thy path. The Lord will open doors.

Focusing on God changes so much in life, desire what God wants for you. He's opened my eyes so that I may see more of him and less of me. Don't go backwards, stay strong and move forward., however as Philippians 3:14 says I press toward the mark for the prize of the high calling of God in Christ Jesus. When the struggle is over, have your mind fixed and focus on serving the Lord. Give God your all using the gifts he has allotted to you. Rejoice and reach out to family and friends and share the hope of Jesus Christ.

Tell others about the love and joy he brings. Give your all to serve and celebrate the one and only who made it all possible. Ephesians 3:20 declares, "Now unto him that is able to do exceeding abundantly above all that we ask or think, according to the power that worketh in us." Jesus is the light, shining in darkness. Because of him I'm at this place enjoying my life once again. Having the signature of God's love is wonderful! The race is not over there is still work to do. There is so much to tell about the goodness of God and so much to live for. He's my great inspiration, and the great I am. I love Jesus and I thank him so much for caring and giving me brighter days.

"I Thirst"

In an atmosphere of praise, I stood to worship God by lifting my hands to honor him and heard these words from Matthew 5:6, "Blessed are they which do hunger and thirst after righteousness: for they shall be filled."

I continued to praise and thank God. I was thirsting after the knowledge of his word, and I was at the right place at the right time. I felt the presence of The Holy Spirit. Just knowing if we hunger and thirst after righteousness, God will spiritually fill us. There have been times in our lives that our spirit has been broken and torn apart. Mixed emotions can tangle you up, and split you apart. God's word can pick you up right where you are. I can recall many days and moments of frustration. When I had to do some things alone without my husband, I was so used to having him around. Having to take the responsibility for things he would normally do was difficult. Crying wasn't always the solution and silence got me nowhere. But a talk with Jesus makes everything right. I had to seek God for myself.

I was the one in need of a blessing and a refill. Praising God makes it better, and it makes a difference. Even when you find yourself by yourself, he's still worthy to be praised. In the word of God it says, "But my God shall supply all your need according to his riches in glory by Christ Jesus."

Not only that, but he also inhabits the praise of his people. Give God the honor, the praise, and the Glory because it all belongs to him. Whether you're in the bed or on the side of the bed; if you find yourself in the spirit, praise and worship God. In your homes, magnify him! On your job in prayer or sitting in your car or locked away in your secret closet. Take the time to offer up a sacrifice of praise, for he alone is worthy. Blessed are they which do hunger and thirst after righteousness: for they shall be filled.

"In Times like These"

In times like these, we need an understanding of the word of God, every minute, and every hour of every moment. Believers must trust the Savior and rely on the promise of his every word. With a sincere heart we can cry out to the Lord, knowing that he cares and that he's proficient! The all-powerful God is an anchor that you can count on day after day. When you are grounded and rooted in God's word, he will provide a comforting peace for all distressing emotions. As we earnestly pray we have relief in knowing that there will never be an obstacle we must bear without him. I don't worry about the assurance of God; I know he will be right there.

I'm a strong woman and there is no doubt in my mind that God won't be there in crisis. I suffered the loss of my husband, an eighteen year relationship and there was no way I could make it without the Lord. My God rescued me at the weakest and lowest point in history of my life. At this time, in my mind I didn't know who was going to save me. No one cared about my troubles. Lacking strength, no teammate, nor husband, I required the Lord Jesus. When thinking back, I'm reminded of the Doctor who was on duty on that day. He came with tears in his eyes trying to speak, yet unable to find the words to articulate. Shaking his head he caught my hand and opened the door to a small room with a black recliner. He asks if I wanted to sit down and I responded no. I told him I had heard about this room somewhere.

Then I inquired, "What's the matter doctor? Did Martinez die? Did he die?" He nodded, "Yes." And I murmured, "Oh my God, my God, it can't be." Crying out to heaven, all I could do was call upon the name of the Lord! My God how could this be happening? My husband! My children! Oh No! It can't be! I have to see him. I don't believe it. I didn't bring him here to leave him. I can't go home, I just can't. The news completely blew me away.

I leaned by the bedside and waited a while before leaving, trying to get myself together to go home. As I sat there looking over at him, I could not help crying. Rubbing the sheet where he laid I was nervous and frighten of what was to come. I held Martinez's hands and touched his feet, checking to see if it was really him. We won't smile or laugh together anymore. My thoughts go to our children, the kids are not here. I have to go and tell them I gave Daddy the last hug and a kiss goodbye.

I walked out looking around in disbelief. People were walking, and jogging and cars were moving. I could see all of this and yet no sound heard.

In times like these God will be your anchor. With the occurrence of sadness and disappointment we petition the Savior. Lying in bed waiting for the sun to rise, I called my mother to say Martinez didn't make it home last night. She said he would not be coming back. I think this can't be right! I'm a long way from home; this is too tough. In these moments, we desire the Savior. Walking into his closet I sat in the middle of the floor just to smell his aroma. I sat there amongst his shirts, coats, jackets, and uniforms. Opening the shoe boxes only for a brief look inside, I quickly closed them in hopes the scent would linger longer. On my way out the door I looked over at a jacket of his that was hanging there. Stopping, I wrapped the arms around my neck trying to imagine getting a hug.

Having to sleep alone without my husband was grueling. I missed him. At times I would climb in bed and hold the bag with clothes sent from the hospital as comfort just to console me to sleep.

Packing up and moving from the place where Martinez chose for us was heartbreaking. Leaving without him was a sorrowful occasion. If we ever needed the Lord Jesus, it was at that moment. As we were departing and turning the corners, I kept looking back until the home we once lived was out of sight. It wasn't until I closed the door that I realized what we had was gone away, and he was missing. I recall looking up toward heaven, it seemed so far away, and crying out to the Lord.

"Bread of Heaven speak a word to me I'm sad, feeling down, and lost. I need my spirit to be comforted! This change in my life is hard. I want your guidance to help lead me. I'm afraid I don't know what to do. I know you care, and I know you're capable!"

Psalms 121: 1-2 utters, "I will lift up mine eyes unto the hills, from whence cometh my help. My help cometh from the LORD, which made heaven and earth."

We're never alone as long as we are depending and calling on Jesus. As long as I live and trouble rises I will hasten to his throne! In instances like these, we need a comforter. When we desire a spiritual connection, the word of the Lord will stand as a fortress. The All- powerful God is an anchor from day to day.

"Pulled Together"

One afternoon I had returned from lunch and while walking toward my car, pull together entered my spirit. I asked the Lord if this is a chapter in my book I pray that a scripture comes with it. Immediately psalms 133:1 came proclaiming, "Behold, how good and how pleasant it is for brethren to dwell together in unity!" This was a good day to work out in the community and share the love of God. Remembering the times my family pulled together to support me, my children got together and came up with a plan. One child would get out my clothes and another would comb my hair. They worked together just for me. My children would discuss amongst themselves who would go out first and who would stay at home, as if I didn't know! At some point in time we all share similarities and need the help of others. Working together shows the love of God. Outreach is a good thing and being present to support someone else is excellent.

God's work never goes undone when we share in pulling the load. One of the most amazing things happened as I was writing pull together. I was trying to remember how I asked God for a scripture. No sooner after this I heard the words Hold on! It was like wait a minute I'm here! Be still and know that I am God. I paused and thought you can't hurry God. There are places in life we must go and in our going we must hold fast for God's help. Hold on even in our darkest hour. In my experience it has not been an overnight process and you will need God to come through. I wanted what I had to go through and what I had to endure to just go away. I desired to blink my eyes and see all my disappointments disappear. Things didn't turn out the way I had wanted. I wasn't in control of my own life God was. This was reality it wasn't going away fast and it wouldn't disappear. I looked to others, and I looked to God. The way he helped me was through my family. His supernatural power took a hold of my grief, and that's how we made it. The importance of family ordered me to be confident in God's word. They had to trust God and see him in me, as a child of his and a mother for them. My daughter came in from school one day and found me crying in the garage. She said "I'm not going back! I can't leave you here not knowing what's going on every day!"

I never knew how restless my son was until I walked into the den early one morning and noticed the television on. My heart went out to him because he was afraid. He told me ever since dad passed away he stayed up all night and slept during the day because he was afraid at night. I was caught up in my own grief and in my own world, so much so that I hadn't notice my children.

I had to stand strong and firm in God. He allowed me to see the hurt I was experiencing in my face. The Lord took control of my life and I took control of my family in the name of Jesus. As we pulled together to be strong for one another we can share the responsibility by helping out when needed. There is so much joy within when you go out of the way just to be there for someone else. Often times it is said that it may be someone else today and it could be you tomorrow. Plant the seed and watch it grow, whether it is in the home, in the community, or abroad. When we pull together, holding on don't seem so bad thank God.

"You Got the Victory"

I was walking to clock out for lunch one day. Carrying my purse and book bag on my shoulder I heard the spirit speak saying, "You got The Victory!" Carrying a heavy load can tear you apart and weigh you down. No matter what is hurting us we must be willing to give it to Jesus. As I was coming out the door on my way to my car, I started thinking about my heavy load and what I could do to get rid of it. If I can stay focused and cast my cares before the Lord I'll make it alright. What a relief to know that God will lighten the load! A breakthrough can come in his word. Come unto me, all ye that labor and are heavy laden, and I will give you rest.

Feel the weight lifted off from everything that held you back. After you put your faith in God you can experience his presence in your life. If you're poor in spirit, you don't have to be that way. Matthew 5:3 says blessed are the poor in spirit: for theirs is the kingdom of heaven. Victory comes when we let go and let God have his way. We carry too many burdens of our family, friends, children, and most love ones. Yet we can have the victory when it's turned over to Jesus. Our struggles can weight us down. They can defeat our purpose and delay our call to serve God. We allow all we carry to instill fear and then try to justify why we don't have victory. We slip away in deep depression and lose sight of God.

Frustrated and heavy burdened can make you feel as if nothing really matters. It was said one day that I wouldn't make it, I was too weak. People said I wasn't strong enough and I couldn't bear the pain. When those feelings came, I cried out. I would say "Lord you know, Lord you know!" I remember sweeping the house one day and I found a clip from the program of my husband's service. I opened it and it read on that eternal day. Bent over on the stairs after reading this I broke into pieces. When you stand to see another day you are on your way to victory.

Once God gives you another chance, smile because the Son will shine! Problems and issues will come, but don't stop moving. I started driving away in my car and it struck me, I hadn't driven in over a year and now I'm driving! I used to sleep on my husband's side of the bed and now I'm sleeping over on my side. There's a good friend of my mother who once said something to encourage me long ago. She said it's been sixteen years for me without my husband and I made it and you will too. I came across her in my fiftieth year and reminded her of those kind words she spoke to me. She proceeded to say, "What are you telling me? It's been fiftieth years for you too and you made it? Smiling and laughing and said yes I did. It took a while and by the grace of God I'm here leading the way for many others. Climbing the highest hills in Jesus and triumphant in victory.

The Presence

The Anointing of God
A Healing Touch
A Shoulder to Cry on
Turn the Light On
Prayer of the Righteous

The Anointing Of God

In the anointing of God, the Holy-spirit reveals his presence. He takes the focus off your situation and places it all upon him. From whom all blessings flow, he allows his presence to be known in a supernatural way. The manifestation signifies change, and that transformation glorifies God. With wisdom, knowledge, and understanding, the Spirit of God teaches strength during trials and tribulations. Thus, this occurrence reveals in us, that he's the most powerful God over our lives. With him, all things are made possible to those who believe and without him we accomplish nothing. I remember sitting in church waiting for the Christmas program to start.

The atmosphere was set to demonstrate the birth of our Lord and Savior Jesus Christ. Full of beauty the performance ministered to us about the joy he brings. I began to think about what I went through and how sad it made me feel. Suddenly, I felt warm oil on my head and through my entire body. I was experiencing the magnificent touch of God. It brought a peaceful serenity and created a new walk in ministry. Many things have made a change in my life. However, most of all the anointing of God gave me the strength and boldness I needed to work. My belief in the power of the Holy Spirit increased, the peace of God covered me.

His power is like no other; I felt his presence all around. No longer was I in me, I now was in him. Chosen to serve in a unique way, God humbles you and prepares you for a greater work in serving him.

"A Healing Touch"

One sometimes wonders if were healed of those things from which we suffer. We often carry and hold on to baggage God has already delivered and castaway. Years had passed, and I was feeling the same old way about the same old things. Whenever I saw others, I would think wishfully wanting my life to have never changed. Entangled in the hurt and caught up in your situation until you can't think about anyone else. If I heard of the trials and troubles of others, I couldn't feel anything. No one's problems, conditions, or hurts were ever greater than mines.

I was in church one Sunday morning, and I would sit on the left side, and I did. Sitting there watching the altar, I began listening to someone speaking about the crisis they were experiencing. It had been so hard for me to understand because I was taken away with my grief.

God completely readjusted my heart on that day. He fixed me where I had been broken, and set me free of all that held me back. Tears began to run down the faces of those standing at the altar. The more I observed, the more I felt something and the Spirit of the Lord touched my heart. I swelled up inside, and my eyes started to run streams of water. I knew the hands of God had touched me. My healing took place on that day in that very moment. Isaiah 53:5 says, "But he was wounded for our transgressions, he was bruised for our iniquities: the chastisement of our peace was upon him, and with his stripes we are healed." God had already healed me, and I had to receive it for myself. One afternoon while, on my break, I was summoned to the hospital for a medical emergency. Upon arrival family members were in tears. The Holy Spirit quickened me to lift up praise to a willing Savior. As we praised and worshipped, we encountered a shift.

We left rejoicing in God for all he had done there and what he had done in me. I was praying and pulling for my family that God would bring them through. I was so happy in the Lord, In spite of all I went through, I could rejoice and praise God for someone else. What a blessing it is to see God at work. One thing I know is that the Lord Jesus Christ mended my broken heart and spirit. He placed a smile on my face. As I listened to the cries of others, God healed me.

"A Shoulder to Cry On"

Walking to my car, I opened the back door; "A Shoulder to Cry On" came in me. I spoke with friends on this day, sharing issues and some of life's frustrations. I remember when I would cry every day, about everything. Good or bad I cried about it. One day the sun was shining, and I cried about that too. It was a beautiful day, and I knew if my husband was alive and here we would do something special. I cried out to Jesus for strength and help that I may stand strong. I've always known Jesus to be a tower of strength to hold on to in life's crisis. Most of us will cry, and that's alright! We rely on Jesus, family and friends, to help us through problems or issues we have. Some Friday evenings I would be low in spirit and the reason because my husband and I would set aside Fridays for all of us to spend time together. We enjoyed being together as a family.

Those days had passed, and because of this, I would come home and sit in the car under the carport and sob. I thank God I'm no longer there at that place in my life. I know my strength lies in Jesus. Thinking of crying on one's shoulder, just the other day, I was talking to a dear friend. He suggested that I go on a fast for three days and seek the Lord about my concerns. Afterwards, he suggested that I inform him of what the spirit would have me to know. A few days later I get a call from him. He's crying, and I'm not able to understand the words he's speaking. So I instantly begin asking, why are you crying? He said I'm worried about my wife it's urgent, I said I'm on my way. I'm trying to get to you, and I'm almost there. Hearing the fear and panic in his voice caused me to get nervous. I'd finally made it there and I ran to the door.

Immediately looking at his face and his eyes I felt his concern because I too had been there I said stop crying and lift up Jesus, drawn by the spirit of the Lord there descended a release and freedom from anxiety and a feeling of joy covered the room. Everything that was said to be was present no longer. I've cried on many shoulders and now others can cry on me. God is incredible! I had ended a day of fasting and sacrificing so I could hear from the Spirit.

My breakthrough was to edify God, even in emotional distress. We are to acknowledge Jesus and bless his name. The bible petitions us to strengthen our brethren. Luke 22:32 states, "But I have prayed for thee, that thy faith fail not: and when thou art converted, strengthen thy brethren." I heard rejoicing in their voices. We draw strength from one another just as we are to bear one another burdens. Hold your head up and let the sweet Spirit of the Lord talk with you. When in trouble, we look to Jesus, rejoice and bless his name.

"Turn the Light On"

Standing at the door, I looked through the glass window where the sun shown upon the church. The beams of light called into my spirit almost as to say, turn the light on. Matthew 5:14 proclaims, "Ye are the light of the world. A city that is set on a hill cannot be hid." When a transformation has occurred in your life, you can't walk away the same. You have to move out and witness for the Lord, telling others about the light of God's word. Countless fall and stumble, making mistakes in darkness from their lack of knowledge of his word. When we study the word of God, he raises us up with strength, power that we may come out of our conditions.

When he does, be the first that shines bright, leading the way for others towards Christ. Tell the ones that don't know the Savior, to get to know him. Cleave to the word and let it shine in you, so that what's on the inside will match the outside. Jesus is your guiding light. He turns the darkness into light. I use to sit out under the tree, with the porch light on, praying and waiting for the day to come that my darkness would turn to light. I so longed for the day that I would get to bed early, so that I wouldn't have to face the dark. When your life is in shambles, and your struggles are prevalent, you wait to shine again. I can say too many that the day will come, and heartache and pains will be over. You can find comfort in God, speak the word no matter what and be encouraged. Moments such as these will pass. Even if the situations differ, don't let it stop you from witnessing about the word of God. He's the Supreme the same today, yesterday, and forever more. Our Father sees us in our dark hour and still delivers. Spread the word, be a light, turn it on and shine for Jesus. His word can open our eyes, and change our hearts, thoughts, and minds. God will transform you in difficult times making and molding you after his will.

Those who follow you can't block the path don't hold back, instead lead the way. Regardless of what's going on, speak a word, and the light is on! Matthew 5:16 advises us to, "let your light so shine before men, that they may see your good works, and glorify your father which is in heaven." Amen.

"Prayers of the Righteous"

The other day I had a general conversation with my friend. We discussed family leadership and how we are to pray for one another. We maintain our relationship with God through fasting and praying. As I listened to my friend, I heard the prayers of a righteous man. Our faith is built upon our trust in God. He tells us how we are to pray in, Matthew 6:9-13 "after this manner, therefore, pray ye: Our Father which art in heaven, hallowed be thy name. Thy kingdom come. Thy will be done in earth as it is in heaven. Give us this day our daily bread and forgive us our debts, as we forgive our debtors. And lead us not into temptation, but deliver us from evil: For thine is the kingdom, and the power and the glory, forever. Amen.

I remembered the long nights that followed my loss. I would walk the floor crying praying to God. One night I opened my bedroom door to look out the room. My mother, who was visiting at the time, stayed at the end of the hall. I looked down and noticed the lights were on. I wondered what she was doing in there. I think she was praying for me. Later on I asked about the light, and she never responded. What she did say was this, I'm praying for you! I mean, I'm praying for you, with all of what's going on right now, I just don't know, with the hurt of losing Martinez; it's just hard to say. After that I got concern about myself and what she said. I began praying to God. Those prayers worked for me, they kept me strong leaning on Jesus.

Sometimes I lived in fear, worrying about if I could or if I would make it. 2 Timothy 1:7 "For God hath not given us the spirit of fear; but of power, and of love, and a sound mind." God has changed me through prayer. I reverence God in my life by showing love and devotion in continual prayer. As we serve and communicate with God, things do change. James 5:16 encourages us that, "the effectual fervent prayer of a righteous man availed much." Of this truth, I know my life bears witness.

The Reason

Jesus is The Inspiration
God's Halo
Talk to Me
In the Light of His Word

"Jesus is The Inspiration"

One particular morning, I woke up with my mind on Jesus. A voice spoke, and I heard, "He's an inspiration." All I could think was, Amazing! In times of fasting we think about the Savior, who gave his life for all by dying on the cross. John 15:13 tell us, "Greater love hath had no man than this, that a man lay down his life for his friend." Though we greatly sacrifice, there is no comparison when it comes to Jesus. God's only son paid the ultimate price, so that we may in him live. He's our shelter in the time of storm. I needed him, as a mother and as a surviving widow.

Many blessings have come through fasting. Our gratitude to the father is to do his will. Romans 12:1 instructs, "I beseech you, therefore, brethren, by the mercies of God, that ye present your bodies as living sacrifice, holy, acceptable unto God, which is your reasonable service." We are to respect God with our bodies presented as that living sacrifice. Withdrawing from that very thing that we desire the most, when we surrender we show our love and faithfulness toward him for his love.

Abiding in him inspires us to know that we can climb the highest mountains and cross impossible streams. Strongholds weakened, and broken. Breakthroughs come and lives changed. I'm impressed and inspired by the love of Jesus in my life. I can raise the roof and shout it across the land that He is an amazing God.

"Gods Halo"

I'd gone into the store to purchase some items. Afterwards, I drove myself to lunch. While putting away the change in my wallet, I noticed, "God's Halo" written in ink on the dollar bill. We are surrounded by wisdom and knowledge. Encompassed by the light of the world, righteousness is a testimonial of the light that shines within us. The gospel of Jesus Christ is the truth and in the radiance of his eminence, he shows us that we are the light of the world.

Walking from a distance, I captured a glimpse of a young woman standing at the crossroads in life. She was wondering which way to turn or what route to take. God shoulders us and he carry us that we may continue to walk in the spirit and ways of his words. The Lord highlights our life with long-suffering and elevates us by the Holy Spirit.

We must be fastened to the understanding that our shelter and safety is in the light. I remember the day when a friend said that my color had come back. I asked, what did that mean? The response I received was I haven't seen you look this way in some time. You look good! I always say I have been through something in my life. Those trying times took a toll on me. I didn't look like myself, no sleep, worrying, tossing and turning trying to make it to the light of day. Those were the times when the light was dim. I couldn't find my way. I was a woman tried by the fire that came out magnifying God. Carrying a light so bright that it outshines the past drawn by the beauty of God's word. His halo shown with brilliance in our life it surrounds us with the glow of an everlasting shine that coats our lives even today. Forever may we grow spiritually and glorify him as our maker and creator.

"Talk To Me"

I opened the door and got out of my car and walk inside the corner store. Greeted by the cashier, she says hello and ask about my day. I responded and said it's wonderful. As I leave the store, the cashier says to have a nice day. I get in my car and drive off the parking lot and heard this whisper, talk to me. I begin praying talking to God. I thought how freely, could I talk with others, who am I? Not to talk with the savior, the very one who knows me best; I can't imagine not having a relationship with the Lord Jesus, the very one I need the most. I'm thinking If I was having a bad day, I wouldn't hesitate to speak with God, but because this was a good day, I thought, perhaps I didn't need to talk right away. It's like God says I'm here with you all the time, I have your best interest at heart. I know what you need, I even know your desire before you ask, converse with me.

I talked with family and friends, about how it felt not having my husband around, but because God knew, I thought, I didn't need to confide in him, little did I know, when. I was weak and broken hearted he was there for my strength, he didn't leave me, and I want forsake him. When I couldn't stand to carry the pain God carried me. I used to lay awake at night and not sleep, always worrying so much about everything, my children, my life and how to go on. I talked to the savior many times, even when I couldn't understand, why? I endured countless, restless days and nights, adjusting to the new way of living. Facing the loneliness of missing my best friend and husband, who do I talk to?

This woman talks to God about everything, each move she makes, why? He knows me best. My every thought, pain and concern. One evening, I was rubbing my legs as though the tenderness was on the inside; it was just the hurt combine with the heartache. Our Heavenly Father knows everything, from the top of our heads to the sole of our feet; tell the Lord where it hurts. He's waiting on us to talk.

"In The Light Of His Word"

I was sitting under a young tree, looking through a book that referenced God. As I was flipping the pages and looking out at the bright sunshine, I heard in the light of His word. As the sunshine bright, it bears witness of God. As we study more about the Lord Jesus, we acknowledge that he is the light. When I started out on this Christian journey, I knew about the Savior and his love, even with insight I still had a hard time during adversity, especially when it comes to the unexpected. I thought just because I served Christ I wouldn't experience some shocking hurtful things. I taught Sunday school, paid tithes and offering supported my church and even so, I had a major change in life, as this widow.

I thought this wasn't supposed to happen to me, I felt exempt because I worshiped God but I wasn't, in studying the word I found out that God is not a partial God he came for us all. Matthew 5:45 states "that ye may be the children of your Father which is in heaven: for he make his son to rise on the evil and the good, and sendeth rain on the just and on the unjust." We serve a just God, it's not about who you are or how you serve or work, this manner of thinking, has no place, if you're in the light of God, his truth should be the strongest image in you, no matter what the circumstances maybe. God allows us to come across many obstacles while traveling down life highway. As we encounter we are enlightened through the knowledge of the word.

2 Timothy 2:15 encourage us Study to show thyself approved unto God, a workman that needed not to be ashamed, rightly dividing the word of truth. As I continue reading more of the word of God, I have the understanding that everything that is meant to be will be.

The Elevation

Lift Him Up
Into His Court
At the Appointed time
Choose This Day
Keep Moving

"Lift Him Up"

Stepping out of the house one day, I walk down the sidewalk, as I'm walking I look around, caught by surprise to see the back window of the car half way up. I open the door to press the button, I turned to face the window and lift him up sprang in my spirit. I thought what a way to say how to praise my God. If the Father has made away, we should raise him above all things. John 12:32 and I, if I be lifted up from the earth, will draw all men unto me.

In my life, I have lifted up the Messiah, publicly and privately, as we speak about the name of Jesus, we keep him on a high level in life. I'm remembering the mid night hour and what it took for me, to see the light of day. I had to thank my God that I came to grips with my reality. Those nights, when I was sleeping, I would awake and see Marty picture sitting on the night stand dressed in uniform, reminders was always around, when I looked over the room, reality shook me, stirring me up on the inside. Realizing this was true, I cried. You can face reality when you lift up praise to Jesus.

Every so often those nights did come; that's when I started to pray, as I lift up Jesus, he lifted me, giving the strength that I needed to pick up my head and raise it high toward heaven, I begin to thank God for the memories and life of my husband, he was a wonderful, caring, loving individual. as I lifted the Savior above the hurt and the pain, he brought out what tore me apart, his devise, drew me closer to him, and whatever I need God to be, whether it's a comforter in the midnight hour or a friend that's sticks closer than a brother, that's who God has been, lift him up. Shouting out to the world, he is Lord.

"In His Court"

One sunny afternoon in a parking lot, I stopped and engaged in a conversation with a friend. We discussed how we are to enter anywhere and grace the presence of God with our daily lives. Entering the job, and places we do go. We should represent Jesus, as this discussion ended, I went on my way, in doing so I heard in the spirit Psalms 100:4 enter his gates with thanksgiving, and unto his courts with praise: be thankful and bless his name. I thought about life crisis and how it sometimes takes a toll on you, it can get hard, trying to always be at our best, is not easy.

In the essence of change, we do become more like Christ as we follow him and grow spiritually. Walking in the newness is to have faith in God. Some of us are struggling men and women, trying to keep up and stay ahead. It's tough to smile or rejoice, when trying to keep self together, constant worrying, about how to make it and survive. Our strength comes from God. Tears of worry would fall down my face. I took a survey, I looked at my life things could have been worse; I learned to be thankful for so much. We have a reason to be grateful, God allows us to touch base with life and enjoy everything that comes with it family, friends, and the joy of just being alive. With a rejoicing spirit we connect with God knowing everything will be alright.

I wasn't always in the best of moods, there were days that I was unapproachable, I didn't want to be bothered, I just wanted my space, although I felt this way, this was ungodly I had to take a different approach in God. However the situation it could have gotten worse, so with this thought I go to God thankful because I realize that in all things I am to be thankful and praise him for he is why I'm here each day not just existing but with purpose, Amen.

"At The Appointed Time"

Driving to the bank, to make a deposit, I decided to make it my last stop, turning in the opposite direction, I heard a small voice say at the appointed time. Running errands, I changed things up differently. All went well and I returned to work. We plan and God directs the path. Everything happens for a reason. Ecclesiastes 3:1 to everything there is a season, and a time to every purpose under the heavens: God is about timing. I remember stopping by my house one day, I ran inside to get some chips, just before leaving, I had to place some items in the storage, well I locked myself out of the car. Trying to get in became frustrating. I'm thinking I don't want to give money to the locksmith. Talking to the Lord about this situation, I said Lord I'm trying to live the best way I know how, even though I was responsible for this mishap, you allowed to happen with me. I expressed to the Lord what I was feeling. I said Lord your word tells me in Romans 8:28 and we know that all things work together for good to them that love God, to them who are called according to his purpose. I begin to thank the Lord Jesus, for keeping me safe from danger seen and unseen. I was supposed to make a drop off to a location for a clothing ministry on that day. Delayed in my commitment, I wait to see how things would turned out, in my waiting; I talked with family and friends. I finally retrieved the keys from the vehicle, I jumped up, waved and thanked God, his timing was perfect. The day I planned to do volunteer work, wasn't the day

God had in mind, He' always in authority and on time. God did it his own way and it was at his appointed time. The very next day, the clothing was delivered, at God's point in time.

He makes all decisions.

"Choose This Day"

After praying, to an all-wise God, I walk into the school gate, instead of disturbing class formation, I decided to stand with another group. It was then and there; I meet the eyes of my pupils peaking at me; the looks I received from them, demanded me to step up and stand as the teacher. I stood with them and placed my hand over my heart in reference to the flag, focusing ahead came this word from Joshua 24:15 choose you this day whom ye will serve. As God's children, we get out of sequence sometimes while serving him. Many of us become too comfortable in our positions and think it's acceptable to step outside God's word and do what we choose, Our Sincerity is to serve God at all times. In this life, we will be toss around, even in this, we are to stand in God and stay in his will and believe for ourselves, when it's all said and done,

Jesus will be standing by our side. As we stay in faith and agreement, we can serve the one and only true God in harmony. Sometimes life circumstances cause tears to fall, remember, we serve God in the good and the sad times. Recalling this moment in time, I share with you this day. My husband was laid to rest on a Tuesday; my family and I attended church service the following Sunday, brokenhearted, and low in spirit; we came to know a loving God in the big screen of the storm we faced ahead. I emphasize, in troubles, in all the appearance of grief, we favor God, and he kept us together as a family. But as for me and my house, we will serve the Lord.

"Keep Moving"

I'm sitting at the dining room table, preparing veggies for a Sunday meal. I had a bowl of onions and celery before me, the smell of chopped onions made my eyes run and the cutting of the celery tired me out.

Taking a break from it all, I went to watch some television, while observing what was on, keep going rose in my spirit. What is it all about? I thought how hard it can be to keep moving when things are not going your way. No one knows how you feel but God. When memories come to mind, the hurt flares and we get emotional. To move forward is to except the change that has come before us; even so, it's not always easy. God's supernatural powers can get us beyond all sadness and depression, just invites him in. In life we want always recognize the need to move forward, unless we are challenge by the unforeseen. In any case, stay in motion and keep on moving, keep living, don't give up on life, God gave it to you, cry a tear or two, God will wipe every one. Put a smile on your face, accomplish what God has for you; be a blessing to someone, allows your strength to rub off on many others. Setbacks will come, that's the time you lean on Jesus. I had some struggles moving forward, I didn't want to let go of my old life with the military. I wasn't ready to move on; when I did it made me sad but strong. I reached out to Jesus, and

I found him in his word, he let me see that I was much stronger than I ever knew. I had confidence in my Lord and Savior, as we move forward; we do see the goodness of the Lord in the land of the living. To advance is to grow up in Christ Jesus.

References

All reference scriptures listed below retrieved from The Holy Bible, King James Version. New York: American Bible Society: 1999; Published May 2000 by Bartleby.com, © 2000.www. bartleby.com/108.

Expectation
Psalms 27:5
Revelations 21:7
Matthew 19:30
Isaiah 40:31
Philippians 2:5
Ephesians 3:20
Psalms 133
Leviticus 25:21

Strength
Matthew 6:34
Psalms 126:5
Philippians 3:14
Ephesians 3:20
Matthew 5:6
Psalms 121: 1-2
Psalms 133:1

The Reason
John 15:13
Romans 12:1
Matthew 5:45
2 Timothy 2:15

Confident
Philippians 4:7
John 14:27
John 15:7
Matthew 5:16
Luke 22:32
Psalms 30:5

The Presence
Luke 22:32
Matthew 5:14
Matthew 5:16
Matthew 6:9-13
2 Timothy 1:7
James 5:16

The Elevation
John 12:32
Psalms 100:4
Ecclesiastes 3:1
Romans 8:28

About The Author

Sharon Outland, a Greenville, Texas native has a deep passion for God which began early in her youth. As a child she grew in her knowledge and love for Jesus Christ through participation in bible training and dramatic biblical performances. She has written a number of plays and productions and is venturing into her latest project as an author. With God's continued grace she is publishing her first book, "It's a walking testimony," chronicling the journey which transpired that established her present walk with the Lord.

Through this experience she came to genuinely know and understand God's love and developed a hunger for his word. She has written, "It's a Walking Testimony" to encourage others to preserver and to lean, trust, and depend on God while walking towards their victory. As she continues to grow, she reaches out and imparts the wisdom and instruction she has received to her co-laborers in her women's mission ministry. Outland also works in her community helping others; she understands that all is owed to her Lord and savior Jesus Christ. She expresses gratitude to her 3 children, loving daughters Sharonica and Octavia, and son Adrian, as they all have given her overwhelming support as she put forth all efforts to release this book. It is with great hopes Sharon has penned her testimony that it may reach out to ministries abroad and tell not only the story of how she made it over, but that there is never a doubt about God and what he can do.